A collection of glass hat pins, pressed and moulded in a variety of colours, and marbled, plain and pearlised. They are displayed in one of Abel Morrall's shop display stands in grey metal, given free with one gross of assorted pins.

HAT PINS

Eve Eckstein and June Firkins

Shire Publications Ltd

CONTENTS

Published in 2001 by Shire Publications Ltd, Cromwell House, Church Street, Princes Risborough, Buckinghamshire HP27 9AA, UK. Website: www.shirebooks.co.uk
Copyright © 1992 by Eve Eckstein and June Firkins. First published 1992; reprinted 1995, 1998 and 2001. Shire Album 286. ISBN 0 7478 0182 7.

Printed in Great Britain by CIT Printing Services Ltd, Press Buildings, Merlins Bridge, Haverfordwest, Pembrokeshire SA61 1XF.

British Library Cataloguing in Publication Data: Eckstein, E. Hat Pins. — (Shire Albums Series; No. 286). I. Title. II. Firkins, J. III. Series. 739.27. ISBN 0-7478-0182-7.

ACKNOWLEDGEMENTS
The authors offer grateful thanks to the following: the Assay Office, Birmingham; the Curator and staff at Forge Mill Museum, Redditch, Worcestershire; Needle Industries, Studley, Warwickshire; Newey Goodman Limited, Tipton, West Midlands; Mrs P. Backe (Norway); Mrs A. Enson; Mr and Mrs M. Gibbs; Mrs S. Hendy; Miss M. Johnson; Mrs P. Jones; Mrs R. Rogerson; and Mrs P. Starling. All photographs, including the cover, are by Mike Pugsley of Harrow, Middlesex. The illustrations on pages 5 (bottom), 12 (top) and 16 (bottom) are by Rachel Beckett.

Cover: *(Left to right) Unglazed blue pottery holder with applied decoration showing lady in Edwardian dress carrying cane and wearing Napoleon-style hat with feather and hat pin, possibly French, and containing: pair of Art Nouveau style hat pins inset with citrine and amethyst, length 7⅝ inches (194 mm), by Charles Horner (hallmarked Chester, 1910); top hat, Davis, Moss & Company (Birmingham, date letter rubbed). Golf-club hat-pin stand in silver with mesh inset in base, Miller Bros (Birmingham, 1910), patent number 24931, containing: tortoiseshell and gold piqué shortened pin; swivel-headed dark blue enamelled square with envelope corners inset with seed pearls; silver tennis racket with ribbed handle, mounted on flat circle, Pearce & Thompson (date letter hidden); two silver-metal lilies; green and blue enamelled stylised foliage Art Nouveau style, marked .925 (sterling silver); blue enamelled bird in flight, on silver, Charles Horner (Chester, 1911). Black vulcanite mourning stand with red velvet base pad holding: halberd in silver, Charles Horner (Chester, 1912); Whitby jet fan head with scene of Whitby Abbey; black composition arrowhead shape with head of a Pharaoh on both sides, marked EPNS. Unmarked porcelain holder with hunting scene, containing: amethyst thistle in silver swirl-pattern swivel head, Charles Horner (Chester, 1911); mauve engine-turned enamelled swivel disc head with patterned edge in silver decoration (unmarked); deep blue porcelain head with silver garlands of flowers and leaf decoration, Charles Horner (Chester, 1906); pale blue enamelled swivel head on silver, Art Nouveau style, James Fenton (Birmingham, 1908). (Foreground) Blue/green enamelled butterfly on brass, three pink paste stones for body; brass 'acorn' style keep; butterfly with composition wings in amber colour, blue cut-glass body, green eyes and paste decoration, marked DEPOSE; and imitation silver covered wire spiral; butterfly in Vauxhall glass, on a 'trembler' (small spring to give movement when worn).*

A sword-stick hat pin (point broken) of twisted silver-coloured wire. The shaft slides into the case when not in use.

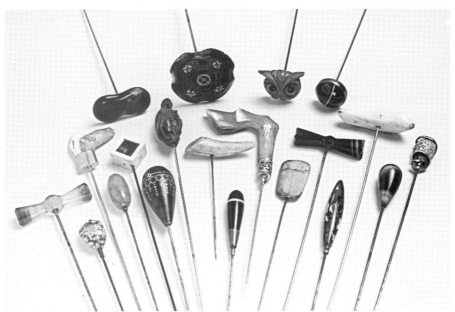

Hat pins of natural materials, including agate, turquoise, serpentine, tortoiseshell (turtle shell), amber, horn, shark's teeth, mother of pearl, piqué (tortoiseshell set with gold pins), carved nut and wood. The pins are of varying lengths. Note particularly the owl's head in Cornish serpentine (top row, second from right) and the banded agate set in silver (top row, extreme right).

INTRODUCTION

In the 1880s the close-fitting bonnets worn by Victorian ladies began to be replaced by hats. By the beginning of the twentieth century these were becoming larger and more elaborate. Hats became status symbols and the addition of hat pins lent an even greater air of distinction to the wearer.

Hat styles were linked to changes in dress fashion. The full skirt of the 1880s gave way to a less cumbersome and less full skirt in the 1890s. The first bustle had appeared by 1870 and was later followed by the fishtail skirt, in which the fullness at the rear of the skirt slipped downwards, producing a fish-like train to the dress. At the beginning of the 1890s the bustle reappeared for a while only to be abandoned by 1895 in favour of a slimmer, flared skirt, which was easier to cut and which in its turn made possible the mass production of the ready-to-wear market.

In order to balance the line of this slimmer-skirted lady, the shape of her hair and of her headgear began to change. During the mid 1880s the close-fitting bonnet, which required ties to secure it, had moved to the back of the head and this necessitated the use of short bonnet pins to keep it in place. These were small glass-headed pins with shafts 2 to 3 inches (50-75 mm) long. When ties were abandoned and hats became larger and heavier, longer and more substantial pins were needed. Manufacturers began to produce hat pins which were not only longer but which had decorative heads. By this time the average length of a hat pin was 6 to 8 inches (150-200 mm).

At the end of the nineteenth century many ladies wore their hair straight, flat to the head, covering the ears and often drawn into a bun at the back. Around 1900 greater width in hair styles was the fashion; the ears were left visible, while the forehead was covered with small curls. To provide width or trimming, additional hair was attached either in the form of hairpieces, which could

(Top left) A small porcelain hat-pin stand depicting John Kyrle (1637-1724), philanthropist, the 'Man of Ross' (Ross-on-Wye, Herefordshire). (Back right) A hat or skirt-waistband pin in the form of a hallmarked silver ski, by David Andersen. (Foreground, from back to front) Four hat ornaments: 1930s pin with imitation mother of pearl heads with brass banding; an arrow with each end enamelled on brass c.1915; painted wooden ends 1920s or 1930s; black French jet (glass) faceted ends, date uncertain. One end of each ornament detaches by a screw or clip mechanism.

be purchased, or made up from the 'combings' saved and collected in the hair tidies on the dressing table. The extra hair was secured by means of a large hair pin or comb, by a ribbon or with a paste buckle or hair slide. A lot of extra hair was needed, twisted or plaited in amongst the real hair, to achieve the more bouffant styles. Ladies' maids became very adept at manipulating the 'rats', as these false pieces of hair were known. A skilled ladies' maid was a very great boon.

(Left) A lady in a velvet bonnet, worn off the face and tied with ribbons under the chin, c.1880, and (right) another in a small-brimmed fine straw hat, which has a high crown with feathers and ribbon accentuating the height, and a butterfly hat decoration (left, just above the brim), c.1890.

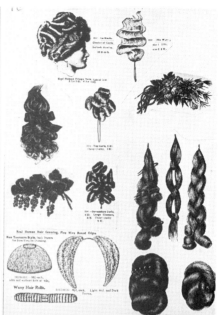

Left: *A lady wearing a fur stole and muff with hanging fox tails, and a large-brimmed and crowned hat with ruched silk under brim. A hat pin can just be seen on the right, c.1910.*

Right: *Various hairpieces, or 'rats', advertised from c.1895 to c.1910: plaits, curls, buns and fine wire foundations. Note the loop attachments for hairpins. The top two wire foundations are for the New Tourneau style for New Empire Dressing and the lower one is a Wavy Hair Roll.*

Below right: *Hairstyles that would have needed 'rats' (extra hairpieces) held in place by a variety of combs, velvet bands and hair slides. Note (top left) the width of the hair, parted in the middle and carried outwards in loose full waves. The back of the hair is confined in a classical fillet.*

The hat pin, or pair of pins, was in the early years of this period pushed through the crown of the hat. Around 1907 hat pins were often inserted beneath the brim, then through the hair and finally out through the crown. This enabled the very elaborate and decorative hat-pin heads of the time to be positioned amongst the bouffant hair styles, adding greatly to the wearer's appearance and to the decorative effect of the hat. In 1911 the *Girls' Own Paper* published an illustration entitled 'The Studious Girl' by Harrison Fisher, showing a mortar-board cap worn with a hat pin stuck through the cap and beneath the board.

Tam o' Shanters, berets and tweed caps were worn for motoring, golf and skating but by 1911 velvet and stitched tweed were highly fashionable for sportswear.

Miss Emmy Wehlen

'Watteau' style hats with eighteen to twenty roses on the brim and as many under it, as well as numerous leaves, were very fashionable. Franz Lehar's operetta *The Merry Widow* was first performed in 1905 and soon the 'Merry Widow' hat was also popular. Boxed sets of hat pins inscribed THE MERRY WIDOW were sold. Lucille, the London couturier who made the original wide-brimmed black hat decorated with feathers and flowers, influenced fashion over the next five years. The public flocked to see the operetta and the dramatic trend in hats caught the ladies' imagination. Hat circumferences increased up to 180 cm.

A studio cabinet portrait of a lady in walking-out dress, possibly French, 1910. She wears a three-quarter length tailored jacket with patterned collar and imitation button and loop on the lower panels. Her hat has the fashionable wide and high crown with ribbon decoration, a large button matching the coat buttons, and a hat pin.

Miss Emmy Wehlen in very wide-brimmed hat (24 to 26 inches, 60-66 cm, in diameter), adorned with tulle and ostrich feathers with a large round hat pin in the centre front. She is wearing a corded velvet coat with elaborate braid and button decoration on sleeve and collar.

From the late 1890s blouses and skirts became fashionable. Blouses with gathered, tucked and pleated fronts and high collars remained in fashion until around 1913. Boleros and short jackets were worn and gradually the skirt became straighter. A new corset, the S-Silhouette, became the vogue and the whole shapely effect was accentuated by the fashionable high hair style. A lady's hat gave her greater individuality, and decorative hat pins enhanced the whole ensemble. Hair-shaping frames, such as the 'Pompadour' and the 'Gibson Girl', and winged hairpieces all helped to support hats which were anchored with hat pins. From 1903 to 1907 hats were tipped slightly forward, then the brim became wider. By 1911 the hat itself might have a diameter of 24 inches (60 cm) across the brim. Hat pins were pushed into the padded crown of the hat and into the artificially padded-out hair.

Hair and hat ornaments. (From top right, clockwise) Hair slide of imitation tortoiseshell inlaid with paste brilliants; hat ornament made from the head, part of the wing and the tail feathers of a tropical bird; hat brooch, composition and paste brilliants, c.1930; pheasant hat ornament of feathers; hair slide in the form of a butterfly in imitation tortoiseshell; large hair grip, metal, 1920s; flexible hair ornament of metal with paste brilliants, c.1900; cockade of feathers.

The hat pins needed to anchor these exotic hats could be as long as 16 inches (40 cm) and the heads were in a multitude of designs. Further enhancing the dramatic effect of the outfit were dress buckles and buttons in the same material and design as the hat pins.

HAT STYLES AND MATERIALS

In the early part of this period hats were often made of velvet with tulle draping, and some had a network of jet beads or lace decoration. Winter hats were made of felt, velour and plush, but straw was worn throughout the year. The straw might be very fine and even finer, plaited straw might be mixed with ribbon in the construction of the hat. Shop catalogues of this period show a wonderful range of types of straw and of decorative straw braid, which came in various widths and patterns, so that milliners had a wide choice, thus ensuring that every hat looked different.

By 1907 a wide variety of hat materials was fashionable, including coloured felt, chiné pompadour brocade, satin in every discernible hue, ribbed shot silk in many colours, and soft velvet with ostrich feathers. Many hats were also encrusted with gold and silver thread.

HAT DECORATIONS

In the 1890s single ornaments for hats such as an aigrette of lace, a high cocked feather or a pair of ostrich feathers were in vogue. Veils had been worn in the early 1890s but these were mostly short and covered only the eyes. A description of floral decorations for hats to be seen at Peter Robinson's shop in Oxford Street, London, in 1905/6 relates: 'Flowers appear on nearly every example of head-gear ... especially white button roses and Shirley poppies ... while pearl fruit and the absolutely charming novelty of a fringe of seed pods are to be seen. Moss is also a great deal employed as a lining to the brim and has a very soft and becoming effect against the face.' As it became fashionable to tilt these huge hats further forward over the face, the space between the brim and the back of the neck had to be filled with even more flowers. The fashion for silk ribbons and bead embroidery appeared to call for more and more feathers, and the wings and even whole birds were seen perched on the hat brims. The tail feathers of birds of paradise and ospreys as well as ostrich plumes were used, much to the detriment of the world's bird population. In 1904 King Edward VII granted a charter to the Royal Society for the Protection of Birds (RSPB) and two years later Queen Alexandra announced that she would not wear osprey feathers. In 1908 an Anti-plumage Bill was first presented to Parliament but it did not become law in Britain until 1921, although a similar law was passed in the United States of America as early as 1913.

REFURBISHING OF HATS

Hats were often given a new lease of life at home or by taking advantage of various postal refurbishment services offered by department stores. For changing hat colour at home Luton Hat Dye was recommended and cost 6d. Ostrich feathers could also by dyed, cleaned and renovated. After the hat was refurbished, as the advertisement in *The Queen* magazine suggested, you could visit 'H. C. Russel's new Floral Salon' and purchase 'A cabouchon of Moss Rose Buds and Forget-me-nots or a Bordering of coloured Cherrie Pie and Foliage' at a cost of 3s 11½d.

A DANGEROUS ACCESSORY

In some areas byelaws were passed forbidding women to wear hat pins with uncovered points. In 1908 the Daily Mail reported that at the Clerkenwell Sessions suffragette prisoners were to appear in court in their hats but without their hat pins in case they were tempted to use them as weapons. In 1898 Mrs C. E. Humphrey, in her 'Word to Women' column, commented on the dangers of the hat-pin point protruding too far from the hat: 'a 6 inch crown

Hat pins of man-made materials, mainly composition (early plastic) and white metal, except the second from the left, which is mother of pearl, and the tenth from the left, which is tortoiseshell.

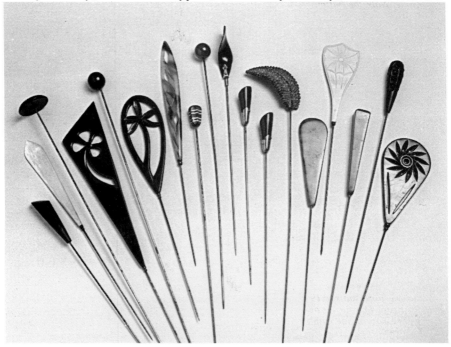

Above: *From a postcard sent in 1907, Zena Dare, a musical artiste, inserting one of a pair of hat pins into her shallow-crowned straw hat. Note the button and silk braid decoration on her dress.*

Right: *Two ladies wearing straw hats and two-piece suits, c.1915. One lady wears a fur tie, the other a stole. The hats bristle with hat pins and ornaments.*

ITS BEST TO BE ON THE SAFE SIDE

SO TAKE

BEECHAM'S PILLS

Above: *Humour associated with hat pins was directed at the extreme size and length of the pin and the danger of its unprotected point, as in this cartoon advertising Beecham's Pills in 'The Lady' magazine, 1911.*

cannot possibly require a 10 inch pin, it is terrible to see the armoury of sharp pins that stick out of the sides of some women's hats.' In December 1913 notices regarding hat pins and the protection of hat-pin points were posted on London buses, trams and trains. Hats and hat pins became smaller during the First World War and by the 1920s hat pins had become as short as 3 inches (75 mm).

Right: *Shorter hat pins of the 1920s and 1930s. (Top to bottom) Mother-of-pearl square made up of different-coloured geometric shapes; white silk composition simulating corded material; hand-painted wood, two pieces with one end unscrewing; black composition with mother-of-pearl insets; engraved and clear cut-glass head with brilliants.*

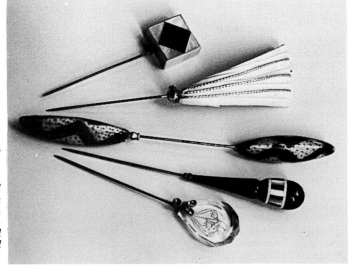

Abel Morrall's factory c.1908 showing hat pins being mounted on cards and in display stands.

THE HAT PIN INDUSTRY

The steel shafts of hat pins were made mainly in Sheffield and in Redditch, Worcestershire. In both areas pins and needles had been made since the eighteenth century. Hat-pin shafts were known in the industry by various terms such as stems, shafts, pins and shanks. In the early stages of manufacture men were employed in the cutting, pointing, grinding, hardening, straightening, stamping, gilding and plating. These were hard, dirty and dangerous jobs, and unhealthy because of the inhalation of metal dust particles.

Once the shafts were finished and polished, women (employed here, as elsewhere, in great numbers because they were paid less than the men) completed the final stages.

One of the most skilful tasks allotted to the women was that of glass-blowing. The flame from a gas jet was used to heat a glass rod, which the woman rotated swiftly to make from the molten tip a round or pear-shaped glass head on the top of the shaft.

One of the line of workers was the 'knocking off' woman, whose job was to reject any imperfect heads.

Other types of head were attached according to their material. Porcelain heads had holes into which the shafts were glued. With silver heads various types of hollow collar secured the head to the shaft. Tortoiseshell and other natural materials were riveted on to a silver collar, often with a double cross-like stud. Other materials were attached by various types of bracket.

Finished hat pins were pushed into papers and cards (pin-sticking) and some were arranged on display cards (furnishing). Other women made boxes, an operation requiring nimble fingers for the papering and gluing of the box. This work was sometimes supplemented by outworkers (often members of the women's families). In the packing department the hat pins were boxed ready for dispatch to wholesale and retail markets. All workers were paid piece rates.

Abel Morrall, of Clive Works, Redditch,

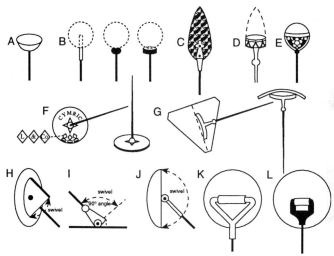

Methods of attaching pin heads to shafts: A, cup shape (often made of brass); B, collars (straight, knopped and flattened); C, rivets joining tortoiseshell head to silver collar; D, openwork caged support; E, elaborate openwork bracket supporting top decoration; F, Liberty head marked CYMRIC and hallmarked L & CO; G, shaft attached to curved support bar; H and I, swivel devices allowing movement through 90°; J, K and L, swivel devices allowing movement through 180°.

Below: *A selection of fancy hat pins from Abel Morrall's wholesale catalogue. (Top row) Hat pins in metal and glass, including shamrock and snake designs, and, below these, glass hat pins with pearlised heads (second from left a very popular shape). (Second row) Three golf clubs, hockey stick and a ball, hallmarked English silver. (Bottom row) Pins with Charles Horner heads in silver assayed in Chester.*

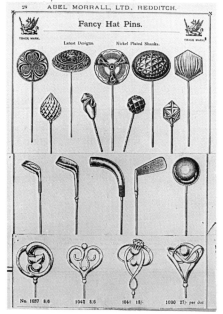

made nickel-plated shafts and advertised their 'Best Steel Stems'. They also had five other named categories of shaft: Bright Steel Shanks, Gilt Steel Shanks, Blued Steel Shanks, Stout Steel Shanks and Nickel Plated Cast Steel. During the 1910s Abel Morrall employed five hundred hands, of whom one-third were probably women; of these sixty were employed in the furnishing room and twelve in the glass-blowing section, while between ten and twenty were working in packaging and boxmaking.

Another manufacturer of hat pins was Morris & Yeoman, of Astwood Bank near Redditch, who produced 'The Portland Hat Pin of Warranted Steel', which was entirely made at their factory. Kirby Beard and Shrimpton's were two other manufacturers in the Redditch area.

Glass-headed pins were made in Abel Morrall's factory, but they bought in other heads, such as silver ones, made in large quantities, mainly in Birmingham. Charles Horner, silversmith and jeweller, whose silver hat-pin heads were assayed in Chester, was also a prolific manufacturer of hat pins. His designs were typified by Celtic swirling interlace, a Scottish thistle, a music clef or enamelled foliage. A number of these designs have hinged heads. Horner used mass-production methods, but his products were always of good quality. As the designs were his own and the whole article was

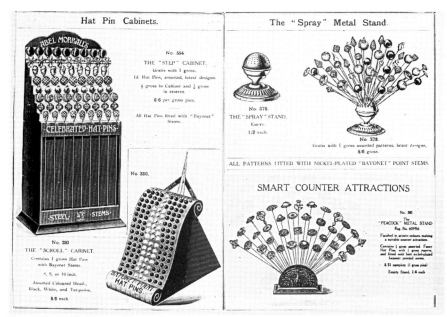

Above: *From Abel Morrall's wholesale catalogue. (Left) The Step cabinet, which came free with one gross of penny hat pins with Bayonet pointed shafts, half a gross in the cabinet, half a gross in reserve at 8s 6d per gross of pins. (Lower left) Scroll cabinet with 8 inch (200 mm), 9 inch (230 mm) and 10 inch (250 mm) pins in assorted colours, black, white and turquoise. (Above right) The Spray stand in heavy foiled metal, showing its capacity to display pins securely and attractively, came free with one gross of assorted pins for 8s 6d. (Below right) The Peacock metal stand finished in artistic colours, making a suitable counter attraction and containing half a gross of hat pins for 8s 11d. The empty stand cost 1s 6d.*

Charles Horner hat pins, illustrating his very distinctive style, showing amethyst and citrine thistle heads. The hat pin top left has been converted into a brooch. The hole for the shaft can still be seen.

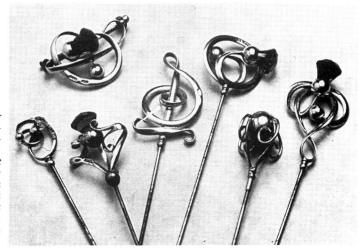

13

An enlargement of part of a Welsh hat in silver showing C. H for the silversmith Charles Horner, and three other marks: (left to right) a lion passant, proving the hat is silver; three wheatsheaves, denoting the place of assay as Chester, and on the extreme right the date letter for the year 1908. Unusually, the mark has been struck twice.

made on his premises, the costs were kept as low as possible. Abel Morrall used Charles Horner's silver heads on various types of shaft.

Pearce and Thompson of Birmingham made a distinctive hat-pin head, often with a hollow circular silver surround containing a stylised flower or animal head in the centre.

Liberty's of Regent Street sold hat pins which were specially made for them and which tended to follow themes of the Arts and Crafts Movement. Some had a dull or antiqued metal finish and others an enamelled background in various colours. They also stocked hat pins designed by Ernest Murrle, a jeweller and designer who came to England from Pforzheim in Germany and went into partnership with a Mr Bennett in 1884 to form the firm of Murrle Bennett. They were rivals, as well as suppliers, of Liberty's. In addition to hat pins, their jewellery included such items as brooches and pendants in gold, and often in a combination of gold and semi-precious stones. Some designs used Art Nouveau motifs. Their pins were marked with the initials MB CO. Some have the word DEPOSE stamped on them, indicating that they were for export. Liberty's pins were sometimes marked L & CO and some were stamped CYMRIC. More costly hat pins, for example in gold mounted and set with precious stones, were also sold by Liberty's.

Mr and Mrs Arthur Gaskin made hand-crafted hat pins in the Arts and Crafts style.

Silver hat pins by Pearce & Thompson, assayed at Birmingham, c.1910.

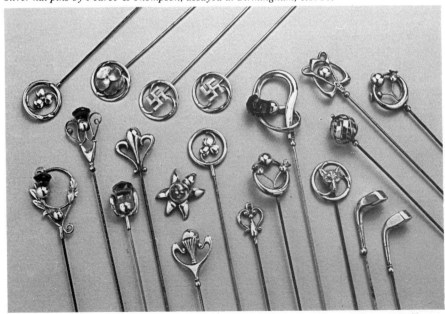

The Gaskins felt there was a need for reform in the jewellery industry, for 'although the production is flawless it is lamentably deficient in artistic quality of design' (*The Studio* magazine, 1905). They produced some attractive linear motifs for their hat pins, which often featured an encased semiprecious stone and sometimes used an enamelling technique.

The English Glass Company of Leicester and other English glass manufacturers also made large numbers of glass pin heads.

FOREIGN MAKERS

René Lalique, the French jeweller, designed hat pins in moulded and frosted glass, for example the four interlocking flying moths, or three locusts with a foil backing to the glass, which was moulded in high relief and set in a gold mount. One of the techniques which distinguish these superb pins is the hand finishing of the surface of the glass to give the correct degree of frosted appearance. They were signed LALIQUE.

Carl Fabergé specialised in making pins using the *plique à jour* technique, where a translucent cloisonné body is used without a metal backing, allowing the light to shine through. Fabergé marks are often in Cyrillic characters.

The Norwegian firm of David Andersen made pins designed by Gustav Gaudernack, who came originally from Bohemia. These were hallmarked with the symbols of a hammer, file and pliers. Both the initials G. G. and D. A. can be found on their pins. Gaudernack opened his own factory shortly before the First World War but he died soon afterwards.

Many glass hat-pin heads were made in Bohemia and exported for assembly in other countries. The firm of Raich Leibowitz manufactured glass hat-pin heads and hat-pin stands in Carnival glass (brightly coloured iridescent glass). The heads were exported without shanks, which were added before selling in Britain at 2d each.

PATENTS

A number of patents were taken out for hat-pin devices. The swivel-head device (patent numbers 21798/23454) allowed the head of the pin to lie flat against the crown

Hat pins sold by Liberty's of Regent Street, London. In front are a pair of green/blue enamel peacocks on either side of an unusually shaped head with thistle decoration (marked 'Cymric'). Behind are a pair of pyramid-shaped heads (one turquoise and one amethyst quartz) set in gold with white enamel square collar decorated with small black enamel spots, on either side of a three-dimensional galleon mounted on a head, in enamel.

of the hat. Devices which related to the shaft and the point include Abel Morrall's Bayonet Point. The patent number 1679 for this was granted in 1908. In 1911 Edith E. Dunn patented her invention: 'Improvements in or relating to pins for securing hats, caps or the like'. Named the Norene after Mrs Dunn's two daughters, Norah and Irene, they were sold in pairs; they had a wire-gauze backing to each head. The point fixes securely into the mesh backing of its twin. It was claimed that the point would pass more easily through hats of fur or felt. The heads bear the patent numbers 15190/11.

The number of patents for devices for point protectors, or keeps, rose dramatically between 1909 and 1912, because the wearing of unprotected hat-pin points in public places was forbidden by some byelaws, so great had been the number of accidents to eyes and faces. A very early patent for a point protector was granted in 1897 (patent number 4412). In 1911 J. Rainsford and G. A. Laughton took out patent number 8657, in which the point had a screw-like

ABEL MORRALL LTD CLIVE WORKS REDDITCH

HAT PINS IN FANCY BOXES

No. E3 Fancy Case, fitted as above, but slightly different designs

EPINGLES A CHAPEAUX AVEC POINTES DE "BAIONNETTE."
ALFILERES DE SOMBREROS CON PUNTAS DE "BAYONETA."

NICKEL-PLATED STEMS.

Tiges Nickelées.   Troncos Niquelados.

BAYONET
POINT

HAT PINS

Patent No. 1679.

SECTION OF
POINT

HAT ORNAMENTS — LACE PINS

FLORA MACDONALD HAT ORNAMENTS

·FLORA MACDONALD·   ·FLORA MACDONALD·

· HAT ORNAMENTS ·   · HAT ORNAMENTS ·

Above: *The balloon-shaped point protector (top) placed over Abel Morrall's three-sided Bayonet Point, inscribed 'Pat 1679' (right), with the reverse side of the Norene hat-pin head (below), showing the wire gauze into which the paired hat pin is pushed (patent 15190/11).*

Left: *Hat pins and ornaments from Abel Morrall. (Top row) A boxed set with a pair of enamelled hat pins with hinged heads and six matching blouse buttons with split rings, c.1910. (Middle row) Advertisement in French and English for the Bayonet point showing a cross-section of the point. (Bottom row) From a salesman's catalogue of the 1920s or 1930s for hat or beret ornaments; one end unscrews for insertion ('Flora Macdonald' trade mark, 1924).*

Below: *Designs of fine tracery by Mr and Mrs Arthur Gaskin in the elaborate style of the Arts and Crafts period.*

end which fitted into a stud-like point protector.

By far the most common point protector was the Perfection. This was shaped like an acorn and was pushed on to the point of the hat pin. Keeps in various forms, from small brass tips to those that matched the hat-pin head, were essential during the era of extremely long pins. In the United States they were nicknamed the 'Jagow-nib', after the German police president, von Jagow, because Germany was the first country to impose fines on ladies wearing unprotected points. Very poor women are said to have used a cork or even a piece of potato as a point protector.

OTHER PATENTED DEVICES

From 1895 manufacturers were producing devices to keep hats firmly on the head. These included complicated structures which fitted inside the hat in order 'to keep in hairpins which reduces the number of [hat] pins needed'. These could be used

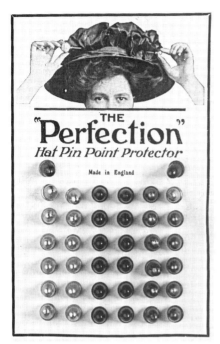

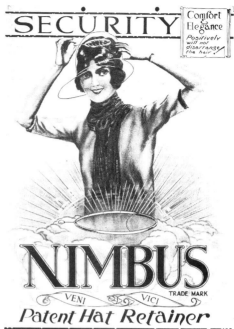

Left: *A shop display card with brass, silver and black (mourning) keeps. The lady with the hat demonstrates hat-pin position and the Perfection Hat Pin Point Protector.*

Right: *An advertisement for the Patent Hat Retainer, another method of keeping a hat in position, allegedly without disturbing the hair. This was done by means of a metal circlet inside the hat, secured by a pin.*

whilst playing strenuous games such as tennis, hockey and golf.

In 1895 *The Lady* magazine advertised the Howard hat pin. This device, which fitted inside the crown of the hat, had two stiffly hinged, claw-like devices which entered the bouffant hair style on either side of the wearer's head. It was claimed that this 'Does not spoil the hat, Does not ruffle the hair, Does not prick the head, Holds the hat securely, Does away with strings or elastic, Is simplicity itself, Fixed in a minute.'

The cost was 2d or 3d, post free, from J. S. Gregg, 92 New Bond Street, London.

In 1911 A. W. Wall and J. Weir took out patent number 9343, in which the pin, 'having had its point pass through the hat, turns back on itself so that the point does not project outwards and be enabled to do injury'.

Also about 1911 *The Lady* magazine was advertising The Perfit Bandeau, a device made of strong buckram and covered with velvet, which fitted invisibly inside the crown of the hat. It 'creates a completely new fit' and was invaluable in windy weather. It was also claimed that it 'can be fitted into any hat in about three minutes, and will not damage the fringe net' (the small hair net which protected the fringe and kept it in place.) This device was an alternative to wearing a hat pin.

Some hat pins required a rotating head, such as those depicting an aeroplane propeller. The patent number 289557, taken out by Sidney Bruce Scovil Kaye in 1912, would 'provide a novel device to cause the object to revolve by currents of air as the wearer moved'.

Above left: *Swivel-headed hat pins in the shape of teddy bears. (Top left) A pair of gilt bears hold logs behind their necks, and below them is a fixed-head bear hallmarked Chester, 1909, in silver and silver gilt. (Top centre and right) Back-to-back teddy bears. (Bottom right) Two swivel-headed bears hallmarked Chester, 1909. (Bottom centre) A larger seated bear hallmarked 'W. V. & S.', Birmingham, 1909. The teddy bear used for hat pins can be solid as well as hollow in construction. The gilt bears with logs are reminiscent of the bears that were used for street entertainment and in circuses around 1900; these designs appear to be a little earlier than the other teddy bears.*

Above right: *A shop display stand in base metal with weighted foot, given away with one gross of assorted hat pins by Abel Morrall, shown here with ten silver golf-club heads (woods and irons), hallmarked Birmingham, 1907-11, and one silver-plated golf club on the extreme right.*

Left: *A variety of hat pins with home-made or custom-made heads. (Left to right) A large head made by a milliner to complete an ensemble showing cut-steel beads and embroidery; cotton cord Turk's head knot; wooden acorn shape covered with checked material; small black shiny bugle beads threaded continuously and wound round a cone-shaped head; two Turk's head knots in silk cord and leather; home-made sealing wax; Turk's head knots in corded ribbon and plaited silk cord.*

18

Ivory hat pins. (Left to right, top row) A pair of right- and left-handed doves designed to sit on the hat brim; five-petalled flower with painted stamens; carved head of a monkey on a fixed hat-pin head; ivory and inlaid mother of pearl flowers. (Bottom row) Intricately carved foliage; plain ivory ball; pair of carved elephants; carved baboon standing on a ball; plain flat head which might double as a letter opener; carved bird; carved cockatoo; carved bear's head.

POPULAR STYLES

Periodicals such as the *Young Ladies' Journal* were advertising hat pins in 1890 in a variety of materials such as silver, gold, mother of pearl, enamel, ivory, moonstone, jet and garnets. Shapes, too, were varied. Prince of Wales feathers, crescents, shells and motifs which followed the contemporary fashion for Etruscan classical-styled designs were popular. Many glass-headed pins, black or coloured and in a variety of shapes, were worn at this time. Later in the 1890s imitation tortoiseshell and faceted steel were in vogue and the French were making heads in gilded bronze with a fleur-de-lis motif. In the 1900s silver and gold, either plain or combined with turquoise and jade, were fashionable. After 1902 the teddy-bear hat pin made its appearance. The President of the United States, Theodore (Teddy) Roosevelt, was taken on a bear hunt. It is said that his hosts were so eager that he should be successful that they captured a bear cub and tied it to a tree. On seeing the cub, the President decided that he could not shoot the poor creature, which became known as 'Teddy's Bear' and began the teddy-bear craze. Bear motifs became popular in all types of jewellery.

In 1905 silver-banded semi-precious stones set in a caged mount were high fashion. Insect motifs were seen in many hats. In 1907 large porcelain and tortoiseshell heads as well as ones of diabolo shape (like a reel but tapered in the centre, following the craze for this children's game) were being made. After the first flight in an aeroplane by a woman, Mrs Hart O. Berg, propeller-shaped hat pins became the rage.

Sporting motifs were numerous and varied, and they reveal which sporting activities were popular at the beginning of the twentieth century. They take the form of

Mainly military and livery hat pins. (Clockwise from top left) Royal Berkshire Regiment, on reverse 'J. R. G. & Son Ltd, pat applied for'; lion's head with 'Canada' above surmounted by a crown, below 'R.N.W.M.P'; glass floral painted disc set in brass; high-domed head showing a dragon and wreath, on reverse 'Jennens & Co London'; lion and unicorn holding a shield with a portcullis and 'Westminster Dragoons' below with 'T.Y' (Territorial Yeomanry), on reverse 'Jennens & Co., London'; a small button with a crown and circumscribed 'North Somerset Yeomanry', reverse unmarked but professionally mounted; a pair of Royal Artillery buttons (also the centre one), on reverse 'Smith & Wright, Birmingham'; a livery button with the coat of arms of the Halifax family with the motto 'I like my choice', on the reverse 'Pitt & Co, 50 St Martin's Lane, London'.

swords, both ceremonial and for fencing; dirigibles (air balloons); ice and roller skates; tennis racquets; hockey sticks; hunting emblems in the shape of foxes and hounds; and even greyhounds. Probably the most numerous and popular was the golf club, with a large selection of both woods and irons to choose from, some with a golf ball attached to the club. A hat pin which shows the head of lady wearing a large hat and with the inscription E PLURIBUS UNUM ('Many made one') around the edge would have been of great significance at the time of the suffragette demonstrations.

In 1911 pins with fylfot or tetraskelion heads (the ancient symbol of good fortune) were reported to be 'selling more than ever, the demand was also felt from Scotland and Ireland' (fashion report from *The Queen* magazine).

Everywoman's Encyclopaedia was sug-

gesting ways that intricate bird shapes with realistic colours could be made from sealing wax. 'Californian Flower Beads' were available for converting into perfumed hat pins.

During the First World War many hat pins worn by the wives and sweethearts of men in the services were made at home from military buttons with the shanks removed. However, many types of button were converted professionally by firms such as Hobson & Sons, Jennens & Company, Pitt & Company of London and Smith & Wright of Birmingham. Another button maker, Firmin, sold attachments for home use.

PRECIOUS HAT PINS

Jewellers such as Tiffany or Vickery's of London would have made and sold bespoke hat pins (made to special order). In 1907 a pair of lapis lazuli pins, and also a sword hat

The reverse sides of brass, white metal and horn hat pins converted from buttons showing (a) professional conversion, (b) conversion with factory-made fittings assembled at home, (c) ad-hoc work in which the pin is usually inserted through the shank hole. (From top left; outer circle) c,a,b,b,a,b,c,b,b; (inner circle) b,a,b,a,b.

Porcelain heads with a selection of different-shaped 'Satsuma' heads of Japanese glazed enamel ware, often on a cream crackle-glaze background. (From the left, top row) Ball head with painted floral sprig; six-sided floral Satsuma head. (Middle row) Six-sided Satsuma head, with mother and daughter; round Satsuma head with butterflies; ball head with transfer motif. (Bottom row) Long-headed floral Satsuma head; dome head; pear-shaped head with hand-painted design; six-sided floral Satsuma head.

(From left to right) A pair of bears' heads, made of moleskin with plaster teeth; two silver hat pins in the form of leaves, one with a frog and one with a cockchafer in the centre, both marked 'Patented Sterling Silver'; black moulded composition with a central banded agate inset; a real bird's foot mounted in a silver collar; an elaborate hat pin, cut glass with silver, surrounded with paste brilliants; silver mounted ammonite fossil; gold interlocking circles with turquoise; agate mounted in silver; rectangular cut glass with silver rope twist mount and enamel key-pattern border; an amber ball with different keep detached; (front) silver and enamel fylfot (a cross with limbs of the same length projecting at right angles from each arm).

pin with the hilt made with an oval ruby surrounded by diamonds and pearls, were known to have been made by Tiffany and were sold in Paris. The Honourable Mrs Alice Keppel owned a hat pin in gold jadeite and diamonds, which was sold at auction in Switzerland for £428 in 1989. Vickery's made an outstanding pair of hat pins in 1906 which became the property of the Honourable Lettice Harbord. They were in the form of an ovoid piece of amethyst quartz with four sapphires inset in gold collets. In 1991 an amethyst quartz owl with crystal eyes was sold for £1000. A considerable number of these precious hat pins appear to have been ordered and made.

Dual-purpose hat pins. (Clockwise from top centre) Spring-loaded removable head for interchanging materials to match the wearer's ensemble, held in a brass surround; ring-shaped head enabling the index finger to be inserted into the ring so that the pin became a weapon, in antiqued metal with green paste brilliants; another ring-shaped hat pin, two metal rings enclosing floral motifs; pin with detachable and interchangeable head (to release the head from the shank pull up the centre knob); flat brass top with initials and openwork mount which slips down, allowing feathers, flowers or a perfumed pad to be inserted.

FAMOUS PEOPLE AND SPECIAL HAT PINS

Hat pins depicting well-known and recognisable people were produced for special occasions such as a coronation or as symbols of patriotic awareness. A photograph of King George V and Queen Mary in their coronation robes (22nd June 1911) was inexpensively backed with cardboard and set into a brass surround. A slightly more expensive memento featured tiny photographs of Lord Kitchener and Lord Roberts, the veteran generals, set in silver mounts. Hat pins with female heads in silver or porcelain have been identified with minor royalty or members of the aristocracy but they do not represent any specific person. The four cherubs from a famous painting by Sir Joshua Reynolds made a popular subject for a hat pin.

Interesting innovations can be found, such as the Mirror Hat Pin set in silver and advertised as 'useful too'; the pompadour or vinaigrette head with small holes in the lid and a sponge inside to hold perfume or aromatic vinegar; a head on the hat pin as a strong ring in which a finger can be slipped, thus making it into a weapon; the Compact hat pin registered by Thomas Walter Farrell of Birmingham in 1909 and consisting of a 'lady's hat pin and mirror combined'. A large safety pin could be used at the back of the waistband of a lady's skirt or on her hat. 'The safety pin migrated to the head and usurped the place of the straight hat pin' — although this statement is not entirely true,

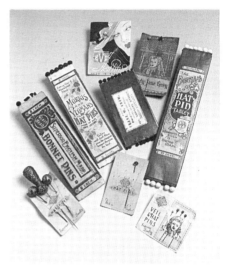

A selection of packaging tablets including a Portland Hat Pin Tablet. Note the use of the term 'bonnet pins' on the packaging, even though they are 8 inches (200 mm) long.

it was described thus by W. M. Webb in *The Heritage of Dress* (1907).

BUYING HAT PINS

Hat pins were sold by department stores such as Liberty's, Harrods, Selfridges and the Army and Navy Stores. They could also be bought from mail-order catalogues. Country drapers, jewellers, antique dealers and even opticians supplied hat pins. Milliners would cover pins to match the

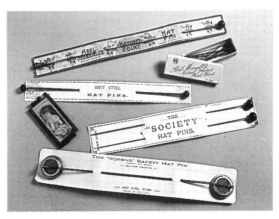

A selection of hat pins on their original cards. (Top to bottom) Abel Morrall's Bayonet Point Hat Pin with keep; a small box of Abel Morrall's Nickel Plated Hat Pins, only 3 inches (75 mm) long; Best Steel Hat Pins; a small tablet of short pins; the Society Hat Pins (these cards all have black glass heads); the Norene Safety Hat Pin, showing mesh backs.

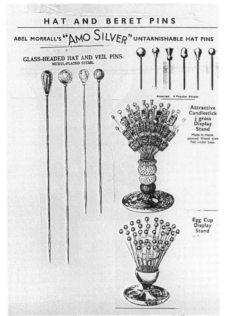

HAT AND BERET PINS

ABEL MORRALL'S "AMO SILVER" UNTARNISHABLE HAT PINS

GLASS-HEADED HAT AND VEIL PINS.
NICKEL-PLATED STEMS.

Assorted. 6 Popular Shapes.

Attractive
Candlestick
⅓ gross
Display
Stand
Made in Hand-
painted Wood with
Felt under base.

Egg Cup
Display
Stand

Above: *Abel Morrall's 1920/30 catalogue for hat, veil and beret pins promotes Amo Silver untarnishable heads in popular shapes and offers two shop display stands: a candlestick in hand-painted wood, of typical 1930s shape and style, and an egg-cup stand in coloured Bandalasta wear, a smooth and very durable plastic.*

ordered ensemble. Hat pins would have been bought as a fashion accessory to complement the whole outfit. Every woman who owned a large hat needed at least a basic black glass pin, which cost a penny.

Although a large number of boxed sets of hat pins do not have a retailer's name displayed inside the lid, boxes from companies like Liberty's and J. C. Vickery's, both of Regent Street, London, are to be found with gold and silver hat pins and their names displayed inside the box lid. Some specialised high-quality jewellers also displayed their names inside, one such company being Ollivant & Botsford, of St Anne's Street, Manchester.

PACKAGING AND COST

Plain glass pins could be bought for a penny each. Tablets (packets of six or twelve pins) could be bought with different-sized heads and different-length pins). They cost from 6d to 1s per packet. A slightly more expensive type was 'pearl pins tinted pink' at $6^3/_4$d, or for 1s $3^1/_2$d a cut-glass head with a jewelled setting could be bought. Gold ball heads were 3s and those set with turquoise cost 18s each.

In 1904 enamel on silver-headed pins cost £2 10s for a boxed set from Scott Adie, Regent Street. The jewellers Parker and Gotte of London offered a gold pair at 2s

Left: *(From top to bottom) A carrying case with white metal cover to cardboard box inscribed with 'Pershore, Worcestershire', and bearing a vignette of Pershore Abbey; dark green leather souvenir case with seaside view; Dickins & Jones packaging box; three retailers' boxes marked 'Z. Wheatley, High St, Abergavenny, Silversmith and Optician'; 'W. Pearsall, Antique Dealer, Goldsmith & Jeweller, 9 New St, Birmingham'; '10 inch Best Quality Glass Headed Hat Pins', supplied by Kirby, Beard & Company.*

Advertising shop displays from Abel Morrall. (Right) The Cone hat-pin stand made of metal, displaying one gross of pearl-headed pins in white and various colours, to be marketed in North America. (Far right) A heart-shaped hanging card with penny hat pins around the edge, and below it the Picture hanging display containing half a gross of penny hat pins for 3s 6d, with hat-pin heads forming the frame around the litho-graphed illustration.

The "Heart" Card, novel and appropriate design, lithographed in colours both sides, with cord at the top for hanging, furnished with an assortment of Penny Hat Pins, best quality shanks.

No. 461.
THE "PICTURE" HAT PIN CARD
containing ½ gross assorted best penny patterns, nickel plated Shanks.
3 6 complete.

9d, whilst gold with turquoise cost 10s and gold with rubies 16s 4d. In 1912 Liberty's were offering 'Yule Tree Gifts' of cast oxidised metal and dull brass hat pins for 9d, so the choice of materials was great. It was socially acceptable for a gentleman to give a young lady a hat pin as a gift, and hat pins were said to be a suitable gift to present to a recently engaged girl.

In 1889 the Princes Restaurant was giving away complimentary and advertising hat pins. And in *The Woman's Weekly* for 26th October 1912 there was a special offer of 500 hat-pin umbrellas as prizes in a simple competition (the umbrellas had a hidden compartment in the handle which held an extra hat pin).

Holidaymakers often brought back a souvenir hat pin and these were available in many forms. The natural material of an area might be used, such as Cornish serpentine, Whitby jet, Connemara marble or Irish bog-oak; elsewhere the coat of arms of a city or a photograph of a cathedral could be depicted on the pin head. Emblems such as the three-leg symbol of the Isle of Man or the Lincoln Imp were available too. Travellers to Japan might return with a 'Satsuma' pin in glazed enamelled ware. Satsuma ware had been made originally by Koreans who came to the island of Kyushu at the end of

Below: *Abel Morrall promotion cards showing women's new independence and participation in outdoor activities. All the hats have hat pins but are shown without keeps. Mother and daughter wear identical outfits and stand in front of an Arts and Crafts style of house.*

Souvenir hat pins. (Left to right) Lincoln Imp in silver (swivel head); shamrocks set in white composition in white metal surround; shield set in a large swivel head; photograph of Truro Cathedral in a silver mount; enamel on silver maple leaf inscribed 'Victoria' (British Columbia, Canada); watercolour of a castle under a clear plastic cover set in brass; Union Jack on white metal surround, possibly a free gift for a liner passenger; two Isle of Man three-leg symbols, one in an enamel circle and one topping a silver butterfly; three heraldic hat pins; a different style of shamrock; stylised leaf with raised stones; silver map of Australia.

the sixteenth century and the ceramic industry continued into the twentieth century. The pottery heads were decorated with enamel colours with gold outlines, creating designs of flowers, birds, butterflies and tiny landscapes. Travellers to Canada might have returned with a Canadian enamelled maple leaf, and those from Australia with a pin with a map outline of the Australian continent, or a gold nugget or kangaroo.

Souvenir hat pins. (Left to right, top row) Indian silver ball head; white metal outline of Australia; dome-shaped hat pin and ring in niello, inscribed 'Bagdad, 1918'; enamelled on brass Canadian maple leaf; Italian mosaic set in brass. (Below, from upper left) Large head in red composition, possibly French; brass and composition domed top from America; large head in red composition, possibly French; Bavarian hat pin with intaglio crystal with a painted swallow in a gilt surround, set in a collar with four garnets and tiny pearls, and with a matching red glass keep; opal and plique-à-jour head in the shape of a sycamore seed; unusual large flat hat pin (possibly French) marked DEPOSE.

A Nippon dressing-table set with an oval tray 9 by 7 inches (23 by 17.7 cm), three pots, a hair tidy (with the hole in the top), a ring stand in the shape of a hand, a pair of candlesticks, and a matching hat-pin stand with large central hole and surrounding small holes.

DRESSING-TABLE SETS

Dressing-table sets were an essential part of a lady's toilet and comprised a matching set of stands, holders and dishes in porcelain, pottery, ivory or ivorine, glass, silver, silver plate or celluloid. The hat-pin stand measured from 3 inches (75 mm) to 6 inches (150 mm) in height and often had a saucer-shaped base which could hold hair pins and buttons, and an upright cylindrical body to store hat pins. The top of it had either one large hole or a number of small holes or a combination of both. The shape and size of the holders varied greatly and they were mostly in pottery or porcelain. Metal stands were quite different in construction, with a velvet pincushion base and a central stem approximately 4 inches (100 mm) high which had an openwork collar to hold the shaft of the pin. The point of the pin would be anchored in the pincushion base. Larger holders for shop displays often had HAT PINS written across them, as did many holders for the dressing table. Display stands for shops were often a delight in the shape of a

peacock or fan in cardboard or metal, holding large quantities of the plainer glass-headed hat pins.

As young girls wore hats like those of their mothers, there were therefore pins and stands for children. These are both proportionally smaller, but in the same materials as the adult versions.

CARRYING CASES
Cases for transporting hat pins when travelling were made of cardboard covered with velvet, leather or shagreen (fish skin). More substantial carriers were also made in ebony and celluloid. Celluloid was patented in 1869 and was often known by the trade name of ivoride or xylonite. These cases were essential to prevent hat pins becoming entangled with one another or the sharp points scratching the delicate head of another pin. Unprotected points could damage the fine silks of dresses or underwear in a suitcase or drawer.

Above left: *Eight hat-pin holders showing the variation in number and size of holes.*

Above right: *The same eight stands, showing the variety of shapes of English and continental souvenir holders from the Edwardian period onwards. (Left to right, top row) Wide-based stand depicting a dragon with 'Barmouth' below, 'Shelley' on base; continental holder with transfer-printed roses and the coat of arms of Boston; holder with 'Wembley, April-October 1924', 'British Empire Exhibition' and Britannia emblem; continental holder with flags commemorating the First World War, 'For right and freedom'. (Bottom row) Holder inscribed 'Hat Pins' with the arms of Penarth, and a Latin motto, similar to the Wembley Exhibition example but marked 'Swan China, England' on the base; small holder with the arms of Petworth, the base marked 'Willow Art China, Longton' (Hewitt & Leadbeater, Staffordshire Potteries); tree-trunk shaped holder with the arms of Great Yarmouth, and the motto 'Rex et jura nostra'; white lustre holder with green shamrock spray and 'Mullingar' below, marked on the base with a crown and 'Victoria' above, 'Austria' beneath.*

Below left: *An open carrying case and hat-pin stand, both in wood (marked 'Ebony') with silver edging and script 'Hat Pins'. The silver on the carrying case is marked 'W. W. Birmingham, 1897'. The stand is marked 'M & C, London, 1908'. The hat pins are a pair of amethyst quartz thistle-shaped heads (left) and a brass ball head.*

Below right: *Short hat-pin holders, possibly for children's hat pins. (Left to right) Carlton ware thistle with Haddington coat of arms; cut-glass ovoid shape in silver mount, with ring-hook collar (hallmarked London, 1914), registered number 631672; one-piece jug-shaped stand (pattern number 2006) with head and shoulders of a lady (this could have held bonnet pins). These holders all contain children's hat pins in gold, silver, enamel, glass, brass and one covered in material.*

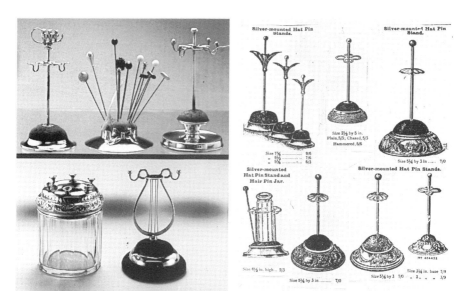

Above left: *Five silver and silver-plated hat-pin stands. (Top row, left to right) Silver-plated stand with owls on a branch with a leaf and two ring hooks underneath, dark blue velvet pad on foot; small silver hat (hallmarked Chester, 1900) holding small hat pins; silver stand (hallmarked Birmingham, 1916) with four ring hooks and dished base. (Below, from left) Unusual glass container for hair pins or hair, silver collar, hallmarked Birmingham, 1909, by 'A. W. P.' (A. W. Pennington, a manufacturing art silversmith and patentee); lyre-shaped stand with two ring hooks on a dark red velvet base with silver lower band hallmarked Birmingham, 1907.*

Above right: *A catalogue advertisement c.1910, with a variety of plain and decorated hollow silver surround stands with velvet cushions inset (sawdust and wire-mesh filled). Note, lower left, a more unusual hat-pin stand and hair-pin jar.*

Right: *A presentation case showing an interchangeable pair of heads with three shafts of different lengths, two brass and four steel (one missing). With the set go three small blouse buttons with ring shanks and five larger buttons (one missing) for attaching to heavier garments.*

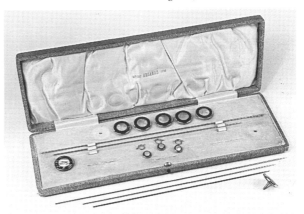

PRESENTATION CASES

Presentation cases were for better quality sets, often containing matching buttons, brooch and buckle, as well as a pair of hat pins. The interior was usually lined with satin, silk or velvet, with loops and individual grooves to hold the contents securely. Retailers could have their trade name and address printed on the inside of the lid.

29

Twenty-one various simulated mother of pearl, sequin, light alloy, shell and braid hat pins from 1920 onwards, displayed in a white metal stand. Ninth from left (upper) is a modern reproduction, or fake.

COLLECTING

Collections of hat pins can be as varied as the hat pins themselves. Some collectors specialise in particular silversmiths such as Charles Horner, with his own curvilinear style, or in certain subjects such as animals, birds, flowers or sporting motifs; others collect only hat pins in one type of material — paste, enamel or natural stones, or even a particular colour.

DISPLAY

Whatever form a collection takes, hat pins look attractive and create interest. They make striking displays in a cabinet or a glass dome or as an arrangement for the centre of a dinner table. Pins could be formally arranged in a pattern on a velvet-covered cork backing set within an old picture frame.

FAKES, REPRODUCTIONS AND REMOULDS

The back of the head of a hat pin should always be examined with great care since this reveals any traces of alteration; look for signs of filing, which may indicate the use of an old brooch as a head, with the hinge and hook removed. The substitution of a new head, often attached with modern glue or jewellery fixative, may be discovered, or sometimes an old knitting needle was used as a shaft with a short and incorrectly honed point. Fake hat pins are sometimes created from beads with small metal separators to disguise the holes. Clasps from handbags of the 1920s and 1930s have also been converted into hat pins.

Reproductions and remoulds, in which the hat-pin heads have been stamped out in base metal, have been found. In the 1920s and 1930s many hat pins had their shafts shortened to allow them to be used in the smaller hats of the time, and other decorative hat-pin heads were converted into brooches and pendants. Fashion has gone full circle: now that hat pins fetch more than brooches, they are often converted back into their original form.

MAKERS AND THEIR MARKS

This list of hat-pin makers, including producers of silver heads and hat-pin stands, is in alphabetical order of their marks. The information is given in the sequence: mark: full name of company: assay office.

Adie Bros: Adie & Lovekin: Birmingham
A. E. J.: Albert Edward Jones: Birmingham
A. J. S.: Arthur Johnson Smith: Birmingham and Chester
A & LL: Adie & Lovekin: Birmingham
ALLd: Adie & Lovekin: Birmingham
A. W. P.: Arthur Willimore Pennington: Birmingham
B & F: Bachrach & Freedman: London
CH: Charles Horner: Chester
D. M. & Co: Davis, Moss & Company: Birmingham
GN/RH: Nathan & Hayes: Birmingham
GS & FS: Saunders & Shepherd: Birmingham and London
G. V. & Co: Gourdel, Vales & Company: Birmingham

J. A. & S: James Allday & Son: Birmingham
J. F.: James Fenton: Birmingham
J. M. C.: J. M. Cheshire: Birmingham
L. E.: Lawrence Emanuel: Birmingham
M. Bros: Miller Bros: Birmingham
PP Ltd: Payton, Pepper & Sons Ltd: Birmingham
PPL: Payton, Pepper & Sons Ltd: Birmingham
P & T: Pearce & Thompson: Birmingham
R & W: Reynolds & Westwood: Birmingham
S & Co: Shrimpton & Company: Birmingham
T. W.: Thomas Wall: Birmingham
W. H. L.: William Henry Leather: Birmingham and Chester

THE HAT PIN SOCIETY

The Hat Pin Society of Great Britain (PO Box 74, Bozeat, Wellingborough, Northamptonshire NN29 7UD) was founded in 1980 by Mrs Margaret Norton. The Society holds meetings twice a year, with lectures, exhibitions and sales at various venues around Britain. Excellent illustrated newsletters are sent to members quarterly.

Fake and reproduction hat pins. (Bottom, from left) Glass ship; white metal shoe decoration mounted on a steel shaft; genuine black-headed hat pin with modern faceted glass bead added. (Centre) Hat pin with black glass beads holding a feather, modern. (Top) Green faceted glass ball, possibly original with fly as a later addition; genuine glass rosette-headed pin with coloured glass bead added.

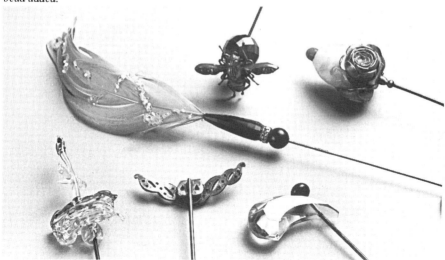

(Top row) Silver kangaroo, hallmarked Birmingham, 1909; white metal dog; lucky black cat, enamel on brass; carved nut in the shape of an ape. (Bottom row) Pair of tortoises in white metal; large silver elephant, hallmarked Chester, date letter rubbed; pair of small ivory elephants.

FURTHER READING

Baker, Lillian. *Hatpins and Hatpin Holders.* Collector Books, Kentucky, 1983.
Baker, Lillian. *The Collector's Encyclopedia of Hatpins and Hatpin Holders.* Collector Books, Kentucky, 1975.
Bly, John. *Discovering Hallmarks on English Silver.* Shire, ninth edition 2000.
Clark, Fiona. *Hats.* Batsford, 1982.
Cunnington, C. W., and Cunnington, P. *English Costume in the Nineteenth Century.* Faber & Faber, 1950.
Ettinger, Roseann. *Popular Jewelry.* Schiffer Publishing, 1990.
Gernsheim, Alison. *Victorian and Edwardian Fashion.* Dover, New York, 1981.
Hinks, Peter. *Victorian Jewellery.* Studio Editions, 1991; reprinted 1995.
Laver, James. *Costume and Fashion.* Thames & Hudson, 1982.
Laver, James. *Taste and Fashion.* Harrap, 1937; reprinted 1948.
Meyer, Florence E. *Pins for Hats and Cravats Worn by Ladies and Gentlemen.* Wallace Homestead Book Company, Iowa, USA, 1974.
Webb, W. M. *The Heritage of Dress.* E. Grant Richards, 1907.

PLACES TO VISIT

Museum displays may be altered and readers are advised to telephone before visiting to check that hat pins are on show, as well as to find out the opening times.

Gallery of Costume, Platt Hall, Rusholme, Manchester M14 5LL. Telephone: 0161 224 5217.
Gunnersbury Park Museum, Gunnersbury Park, Popes Lane, London W3 8LQ. Telephone: 020 8992 1612.
Museum of Costume, Assembly Rooms, Bennett Street, Bath BA1 2QH. Telephone: 01225 477789. Website: www.museumofcostume.co.uk
Victoria and Albert Museum, Cromwell Road, South Kensington, London SW7 2RL. Telephone: 020 7942 2000. Website: www.vam.ac.uk
Worcestershire County Museum, Hartlebury Castle, Hartlebury, near Kidderminster, Worcestershire DY11 7XZ. Telephone: 01299 250416.
York Castle Museum, Eye of York, York YO1 9RY. Telephone: 01904 653611. Website: www.york.gov.uk/heritage/museums/castle